My First Book of
Dinosaurs

ALL ABOUT PREHISTORIC CREATURES FOR KIDS

ERIN WATERS, MEd

ROCKRIDGE
PRESS

To Billy, Teddy, and Annie—you are the most dino-mite crew. I love you!

First Rockridge Press edition 2023

Rockridge Press and the Rockridge Press logo are trademarks or registered trademarks of Callisto Media Inc. and/or its affiliates in the United States and other countries and may not be used without written permission.

For general information on our other products and services, please contact our Customer Care Department within the United States at (866) 744-2665, or outside the United States at (510) 253-0500.

Paperback ISBN: 979-8-88608-772-7
eBook ISBN: 979-8-88650-233-6

Manufactured in the United States of America

Series Designer: Sean Doyle
Interior and Cover Designer: Jennifer Hsu
Art Producer: Hannah Dickerson
Editor: Laura Bryn Sisson
Production Editor: Jael Fogle
Production Manager: Martin Worthington

Illustrations © Annalisa and Marina Durante
Author photo courtesy of Me and the Moon Photography

10 9 8 7 6 5 4 3 2 1 0

This book belongs to

_____

Yangchuanosaurus

What Is a Dinosaur?

Dinosaurs lived on Earth a very long time ago—before people and the animals we know today.

Dinosaurs were land animals. They were reptiles like lizards and snakes. There were many different types of dinosaurs.

Dinosaurs weren't all alive at the same time. Some lived in the Triassic Period, when dinosaurs first appeared on Earth. Some dinosaurs lived during the Jurassic Period. Others lived in the Cretaceous Period, the last time dinosaurs were alive. Dinosaurs are now extinct, which means they are *all* no longer alive.

Carnivores

Some dinosaurs were carnivores. Carnivores are animals that eat other animals, like lions do today. Dinosaurs like *Megalosaurus* often ate other dinosaurs! Dinosaurs that were carnivores usually had sharp, pointy teeth and claws for catching and eating animals. Some carnivorous dinosaurs were big, like *Tyrannosaurus*, but others were small, like *Velociraptor*!

Herbivores

Some dinosaurs were **herbivores**. Herbivores are animals that eat plants. Plant-eating dinosaurs ate things like leaves, pine needles, and bushes. Herbivore dinosaurs had wide, flat teeth that they used to chew tough plants. Some herbivores, like *Argentinosaurus*, had long necks for reaching leaves in high trees.

Argentinosaurus

Henodus

Underwater Creatures

Although many dinosaurs roamed the land, other prehistoric creatures swam the seas. These sea beasts were not *actually* dinosaurs. One of these underwater creatures was *Megalodon,* a family member of today's great white shark. It was as big as two fire trucks facing bumper to bumper! *Henodus* was another prehistoric creature that lived underwater. This reptile was much smaller. It had a tough shell to protect from predators.

Confuciusornis (left), Microraptor (right)

Flying Creatures

Most dinosaurs could not fly, but they lived with some amazing prehistoric creatures that could. Two of these creatures were *Confuciusornis* and *Microraptor*. *Confuciusornis* was a prehistoric bird. *Microraptor* was a small dinosaur with wings. Pterosaurs were another group of flying creatures. These flying reptiles *looked* a lot like dinosaurs but were in a different family. They were like cousins to the dinosaurs.

Coelophysis

see-low-FY-sis

Coelophysis was a small, fast hunter with sharp teeth. They traveled together in groups. *Coelophysis* ate fish, reptiles, and insects. Scientists know a lot about this dinosaur because they studied *Coelophysis* bones found at a ranch in New Mexico, USA. Scientists who study dinosaur bones are called **paleontologists**.

When: Late Triassic/Early Jurassic Period

Where: The forests of Arizona and New Mexico in the United States, and maybe Africa

Length: 10 feet

Height: 3 feet

Weight: 40 pounds

Coelophysis *was a family-loving dinosaur!*
Grown-ups and babies lived together just like
many of us live at home with our families.

Herrerasaurus *had very short arms! Its secret weapon was the claws on each hand that it used to grab the animals it hunted.*

Herrerasaurus

huh-RARE-uh-SAWR-us

Herrerasaurus was the size of a lion and was as fierce as one, too. It was the biggest of all the meat-eating dinosaurs of its time! *Herrerasaurus* lived in the jungle and ate reptiles and other small dinosaurs. It had ten toes but used only six of them to walk.

When: Late Triassic Period
Where: Forests in Argentina
Length: 13 feet
Height: 5.5 feet
Weight: 700 pounds

Mussaurus

moos-SAWR-us

Mussaurus means "mouse lizard." It was named this because the first bones scientists found were from a baby that could fit in the palm of your hand! Scientists think adult *Mussauruses* were *actually* the size of a pickup truck. *Mussaurus* walked on four legs and was probably a fast dinosaur that used its speed to escape other dinosaurs.

When: Late Triassic Period
Where: Forests in Argentina
Length: 20 feet
Height: 6 feet
Weight: 2,000 pounds

Mussauruses *lived and traveled with other* Mussauruses *their same age and size.*

Plateosaurus *means* "broad lizard." It had very wide shoulders!

Plateosaurus

PLAY-tee-uh-SORE-us

Plateosaurus was the largest and heaviest dinosaur alive during its time on Earth. It had teeth that could chew through the toughest leaves, so it ate many kinds of plants. *Plateosaurus* walked on all fours but could stand up on two legs to reach branches. It had a long tail that it used as a weapon.

When: Late Triassic Period
Where: Forests in South Africa
Length: 26 feet
Height: 12 feet
Weight: 8,000 pounds

Caelestiventus

say-LESS-tah-VIN-tuss

Caelestiventus was a flying reptile that lived in the desert. This creature was the size of a cat and had over 100 pointy teeth. Scientists think it ate insects and small lizards. *Caelestiventus* is hard to study because its bones were very **fragile** and did not easily turn into **fossils**, the remains of animals from long ago that have become rocks.

When: Late Triassic Period

Where: Western United States

Length: 7 to 8 inches long, but its **wingspan** (wing from tip to tip) measured 5 feet long

Height: 1 foot

Weight: 8 pounds

Scientists think that Caelestiventus *was the first flying prehistoric creature to live in the desert.*

Atopodentatus *was as long as an alligator!*

Atopodentatus

ah-TOP-oh-DEN-ta-tuss

Atopodentatus was a **marine** reptile, which means it swam the seas. Unlike most large marine animals, *Atopodentatus* was a prehistoric ocean creature that did not eat meat. Its name means "strange tooth" because its teeth were shaped like a zipper! *Atopodentatus* had a snout that worked like a vacuum cleaner it used to eat **algae** off the ocean floor.

When: Middle Triassic Period
Where: China
Length: About 10 feet
Height: 3 feet
Weight: 150 pounds

Allosaurus
AL-oh-SAWR-us

Allosaurus was not only super big but also very fast. This meat eater could run nearly 40 miles per hour! *Allosaurus* was as big as a bus and ate herbivore dinosaurs of all sizes. It had powerful arms and claws that it used to catch **prey**, an animal that is eaten as food.

When: Late Jurassic Period

Where: In the United States (Colorado, New Mexico, Utah, and Wyoming) and Portugal

Length: 39 feet

Height: 16 feet

Weight: 6,000 pounds

One of Allosaurus's *favorite meals* was the Stegosaurus. Scientists have found fossils from both dinosaurs that showed signs of battle with each other.

Dilophosaurus's *top teeth were twice as long as its bottom teeth. It had 33 teeth in all, and most of them were curved instead of straight.*

Dilophosaurus

dye-LOAF-oh-SAWR-us

Dilophosaurus was a meat eater the size of an SUV! Scientists think it ate animals like baby crocodiles, small dinosaurs, and fish. *Dilophosaurus*'s arms could not move much, but it had a small hook on its jaw to help catch slippery animals like fish.

When: Early Jurassic Period
Where: Forests in Arizona
Length: 23 feet
Height: 5 feet
Weight: 880 pounds

Megalosaurus

MEG-uh-low-SAWR-us

Megalosaurus means "big reptile," which scientists chose because it was the size of a school bus! This dinosaur had four legs like a crocodile, but it actually walked on its back two legs. Because of its size, *Megalosaurus* could hunt animals of all sizes. *Megalosaurus* scratched trees to make its claws extra sharp, much like bears do today.

When: Middle Jurassic Period
Where: Forests and shores of England
Length: 30 feet
Height: 10 feet
Weight: 4,500 pounds

Paleontologists used to think that Megalosaurus hunted its prey and also stole food from smaller dinosaurs.

Brachiosaurus *was as tall as a three-story building!*

Brachiosaurus

BRAK-ee-oh-SAWR-us

Brachiosaurus used its long neck to eat leaves from trees. It had some **unique** features—it had a nose on top of its head that it may have used like a snorkel when its body was in the water, and its teeth were shaped like spoons. *Brachiosaurus* was tall and super heavy—it weighed more than eighteen elephants!

When: Late Jurassic Period

Where: United States (Colorado and Utah) and Tanzania

Length: 70 feet

Height: 30 feet

Weight: 115,000 pounds

Stegosaurus

STEG-oh-SAWR-us

Stegosaurus was a huge dinosaur that walked on four legs. The name *Stegosaurus* means "roof lizard." It had bony **plates** on its back that look like the tiles on a roof. *Stegosaurus* had spikes on its tail that it would swing any time it needed protection. It was a plant eater.

When: Jurassic Period, Cretaceous Period

Where: North America

Length: Up to 29 feet (as long as one school bus)

Height: Grew to a height of 14 feet (same as a small giraffe)

Weight: Between 5 to 7 tons (as heavy as a delivery truck)

Scientists believe that the plates on Stegosaurus's back may have been used to capture the sunrays. This would have helped warm the dinosaur.

Scientists studied the bones of Archaeopteryx and found that, although it had wings, it probably could glide only short distances.

Archaeopteryx

ahr-key-OP-tur-icks

Archaeopteryx was a small meat-eating dinosaur with wings and feathers, but it probably couldn't fly. Scientists used *Archaeopteryx*'s fossil to learn that today's birds came from the dinosaur family. *Archaeopteryx* was the size of a crow. It used its claws to climb trees and then glide to another tree using its wings.

When: Late Jurassic Period

Where: Germany

Length: 20 inches

Height: 15 inches

Weight: 1.8 to 2.2 pounds

Wingspan: 2 feet

Pterodactylus
tare-o-DACK-tull-us

When *Pterodactylus* fossils were found, scientists did not know what kind of animal it was. Some thought it was a sea creature or a flying marsupial—the same family as kangaroos. Now scientists know that *Pterodactylus* was a pterosaur, a flying reptile that was like a cousin of the dinosaurs.

When: Late Jurassic Period
Where: Germany
Length: 2 feet
Weight: 2 pounds
Wingspan: 3 feet

Pterodactylus *had no teeth! Instead, it used its beak to grab fish and open clams to eat.*

Dakosaurus *was as long as a soccer goalpost and about as heavy as three horses.*

Dakosaurus

DAH-ko-SORE-us

Dakosaurus was a marine crocodile that lived in the ocean. *Dakosaurus* means "biter lizard." It had big teeth that were sharp like knives. This creature had four short flippers and a very powerful tail to swim through the water and catch prey.

When: Late Jurassic to Early Cretaceous Periods
Where: Europe and South America
Length: 15 feet
Height: 2 feet
Weight: 2,000 pounds

Baryonyx

BARE-ee-ON-icks

Baryonyx was a large carnivore that fed on fish, turtles, and plant-eating dinosaurs. It had huge claws and ninety-five long, sharp teeth. *Baryonyx* was the size of a school bus and had a head shaped like an alligator's. This dinosaur spent a lot of time in the water.

When: **Early Cretaceous Period**
Where: **Spain and England**
Length: **32 feet**
Height: **8 feet**
Weight: **2,700 pounds**

Baryonyx *means "heavy claw." Its claws were as long as a big soda bottle!*

Deinonychus *had a large brain compared to other dinosaurs, and scientists think it may have been one smart dinosaur!*

Deinonychus

dye-NON-ih-kus

Deinonychus was the size of a tiger, and fast like one, too! This warm-blooded predator had feathers. It had sharp teeth to tear off pieces of meat from the prey it caught. *Deinonychus* also had sharp claws and eyes that worked like binoculars, which helped it spot prey easily.

When: Early Cretaceous Period
Where: Utah
Length: 13 feet
Height: 3 feet
Weight: 150 pounds

Tyrannosaurus

tie-RAN-oh-SAWR-us

Tyrannosaurus rex's name means "king of the terrible lizards." *Tyrannosaurus rex*, or *T. rex* for short, was a fierce carnivore that hunted other dinosaurs. It had jaws strong enough to crush any animal it ate. *T. rex* grew as tall as a two-story house, with each of its teeth as long as a banana!

When: Late Cretaceous Period

Where: Forests and rivers of western North America

Length: 41 feet

Height: 12 feet (like two refrigerators stacked on top of each other)

Weight: 15,000 pounds (the weight of about eight cars)

Scientists believe the female Tyrannosaurus *was larger than the male, probably to protect her babies.*

The Utahraptor *was named after where it was found—Utah in the United States!*

Utahraptor

YOU-taw-RAP-tur

Utahraptor was one of the smartest and most dangerous meat-eating dinosaurs. It had strong arms and long claws to grab onto prey and shred it apart. Its foot claw was super sharp and long—the same as two pencils laid end to end! *Utahraptor* was one of the biggest and strongest of all **raptors**.

When: Cretaceous Period

Where: Forests and beaches in the United States (Utah)

Length: 23 feet

Height: 8 feet

Weight: 2,000 pounds

Velociraptor

vuh-LAH-su-RAP-tor

Velociraptor was a small birdlike dinosaur with feathers. Even though it was the size of a large turkey and had feathered arms that looked like wings, *Velociraptor* could not fly. *Velociraptors* had more than 100 teeth, but their greatest power came from their large back feet with giant claws.

When: Cretaceous Period

Where: Asia

Length: 6 feet (about as long as a bed)

Height: 2 feet (about the same as a big chicken)

Weight: 35 pounds (the size of a 4-year-old)

Velociraptor *means "fast thief."* It had a speedy way of attacking its prey.

Ankylosaurus *had teeth that were shaped like leaves! Each tooth had bumpy edges that made it easier to pluck plants off the ground to eat.*

Ankylosaurus

an-KIE-low-SAWR-us

Ankylosaurus was an **armored** dinosaur, which means it had bones in its skin so that no predator could bite through it. This dinosaur had a tail with a club at the end made of solid bone! *Ankylosaurus* lived at the end of the Cretaceous Period, right before an **asteroid** struck and caused all dinosaurs to become extinct.

When: Cretaceous Period

Where: Forests and swamps in the United States (Montana and Wyoming) and Canada

Length: 30 feet

Height: 8 feet

Weight: 18,000 pounds

Iguanodon

ig-WAN-oh-DON

Iguanodon was one of the of the first dinosaurs ever found by paleontologists. Its name means "iguana tooth." Its teeth were shaped like an iguana's teeth. *Iguanodon* had a large thumb spike on each hand, which it probably used as a weapon. This dinosaur could walk on two legs or four.

When: Early Cretaceous Period

Where: Europe, China, and South America

Length: 43 feet

Height: 10 feet

Weight: 7,500 pounds

Scientists think Iguanodon *might have had a long tongue like a giraffe.*

Parasaurolophus's *teeth fell out and grew back many times during its life.*

Parasaurolophus

PAIR-uh-SAWR-ohl-OW-fuss

Parasaurolophus was a plant eater the size of a school bus! This dinosaur had a giant **crest** on its head. Most scientists think *Parasaurolophus* used this crest to make loud noises to scare away predators. *Parasaurolophus* had a bill that made it *look* like a duck, but it spent more time in the forest than it did in the water.

When: Late Cretaceous Period

Where: United States (Utah and New Mexico) and Canada

Length: 33 feet

Height: 12 feet

Weight: 5,000 pounds

Triceratops

try-SER-uh-tops

Triceratops was a plant-eating dinosaur that weighed as much as five rhinoceroses. Even though it was large, *Triceratops* could run fast. *Triceratops* means "three-horned face." It had two brow horns and one nose horn on its head. Triceratops used its teeth to cut through leaves and could also regrow teeth it lost.

When: Late Cretaceous Period

Where: Forests and swamps in Western United States and Canada

Length: 30 feet

Height: 12 feet

Weight: 25,000 pounds

Triceratops *had one of the largest heads ever found on a land animal!*

Pteranodons *lived near the sea.*
Scientists think that they swooped into
the water and ate fish and crabs.

Pteranodon

ta-RAN-oh-don

Pteranodons were fish-eating pterosaurs, which were large flying creatures. Female *Pteranodons* were about half the size of males. Also, males had a crest on the back of their heads and females did not. All *Pteranodons* had very large wingspans.

When: Late Cretaceous Period
Where: North America
Length: Wingspan of 22 feet
Height: 6 feet
Weight: 35 pounds

Quetzalcoatlus

KET-zul-koh-AH-tul-us

Possibly the largest flying animal ever to live on Earth, *Quetzalcoatlus* was about the size of a giraffe! Scientists agree that *Quetzalcoatlus* was a meat eater but aren't exactly sure what it ate. Some think it ate fish and other small sea animals, and others think it ate baby dinosaurs. It's also possible it fed on dead dinosaurs, much like a vulture!

When: Late Cretaceous Period

Where: Western United States

Length: Wingspan of 40 feet (the same as a fighter jet!)

Weight: 155 pounds

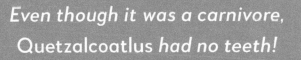

*Even though it was a carnivore,
Quetzalcoatlus had no teeth!*

Allosaurus

Trilobites

Allosaurus

Pterodactylus

Dinosaurs and You

Learning about dinosaurs helps us understand more about our world. Studying dinosaurs shows us important connections between life long ago and today. Dinosaurs also give us clues about **modern** animals because so many animals today come from the dinosaur family.

Keep learning about these fascinating creatures! You could be a paleontologist when you grow up.

GLOSSARY

ALGAE: Plantlike living things usually found in water

ARMORED: Protected

ASTEROID: A rocky object in space

CARNIVORES: Animals that eat other animals

CREST: A crop of hair, bone, feathers, or fur on top of an animal's head

CRETACEOUS PERIOD: The period after the Jurassic Period, the last time dinosaurs were alive on Earth, from 145 million years ago to 66 million years ago

EXTINCT: No longer alive on Earth

FOSSILS: The remains or traces of things that lived long ago

FRAGILE: Easily breakable

HERBIVORES: Animals that eat plants

JURASSIC PERIOD: The period on Earth between the Triassic and Cretaceous Periods, from 201 million years ago to 145 million years ago

MARINE: Found in the sea

MARSUPIALS: Animals known for carrying their babies in a pouch

MODERN: The present time or not long ago

PALEONTOLOGISTS: Scientists who study fossils

PLATES: Thin, flat body parts made of bone

PREDATORS: Animals that live by hunting, killing, and eating other animals

PREHISTORIC: A time before history was written down by humans

PREY: An animal that is hunted or eaten by another animal for food

PTEROSAURS: Flying reptiles that lived in the Jurassic and Cretaceous Periods

RAPTORS: Large birds of prey

REPTILES: Cold-blooded animals usually covered in scales or plates

TRIASSIC PERIOD: The period on Earth when dinosaurs first appeared, from 252 million years ago to 201 million years ago

UNIQUE: One of a kind

WINGSPAN: The distance from the tip of a wing to the tip of another wing

ABOUT THE AUTHOR

 **ERIN WATERS, MEd**, is a first grade teacher turned curriculum designer who uses her talents and knowledge to create games and resources for elementary classrooms. Erin lives in Ohio with her husband and two children, Teddy and Annie. When she isn't creating, Erin loves to read, craft, cook, and enjoy family time.

ABOUT THE ILLUSTRATORS

 **ANNALISA AND MARINA DURANTE** are twin sisters, naturalistic illustrators, and artists. Their illustrations have been published in books in many countries around the world, and they have won several prestigious prizes in national and international naturalistic art competitions.